LYRICS

TO A WOMAN

IN HARLEM

A Book of Poetry

T Y R O N   M O T I F

LYRICS TO A WOMAN IN HARLEM

Copyright © 2015 Tyron Ross (Tyron Motif)

Printed in the United States of America

ISBN-13:978-0692386705

ISBN-10:069238670X

Printed by Createspace 2015

Published by BlaqRayn Publishing Plus 2015

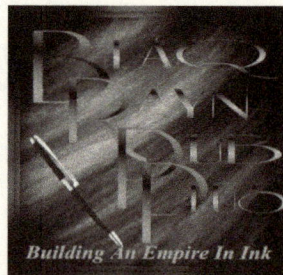

Building An Empire In Ink

DEDICATION

This book is dedicated to my grandmother,
Annett Ross
Without the life lessons and values she instilled
me
I would not be alive today.
Rest forever in peace

Also to my children
Tyron and Tymir
You both are the reason why I write.
You help me to inspire your generation to push
forward
Regardless of what tomorrow may bring
I love you both dearly!

Foreword

"*Lyrics To A Woman In Harlem*", as the title would have you to assume, that it is inspired by a woman. This collection of poetry written by New York based author Tyron Motif is indeed inspired by a woman, many women, and women of color to be exact. As he emphatically connects with the "black" woman through her heart, mind and soul, his pen pours out admiration, love, respect, honor and gratitude for the women he encountered and to those like them.

With love being the base to this book, you'll find many other genres in which most reflects Tyron speaking to/of his muse. Whether it be a dose of erotica, dedication and storytelling or to pedestal with praise there will be no guessing to where his inspiration derived. In his unique voice he sets the air free flowing and breezy, yet sometimes heavy winded as he conveys experiences, ideas, or emotions in a vivid and imaginative way. There are many layers as you will discover hidden jewels in this collection such as **"Buried Treasures Beneath Harlem"**, **"Smothered by Certainty"** **"Gold Tips"**, **"BooBoo Love Juice"**, inspiring the book title "*Lyrics To A Woman In Harlem*" and so many more unmentioned.

Privileged to meet Tyron Motif on a social website last year, in 2014, I have grown to admire and respect his creativity. Once you read his book of poetry, *"Lyrics To A Woman In Harlem"*, I have no doubt that you too will be in awe of his work. Each poem featured is unique and yet enriched with heartfelt ink that will leave with the reader a taken back feeling and warmth. For each poem is also a journey and as you travel by fingertips and eyes, you will not want this excursion to end. Tyron Motif's *"Lyrics To A Woman In Harlem"* is a definite must have addition to your poetic library.

Shantelle 'Elle' McLin
Author/Poet, Website Administrator, & Photographer

Table of Contents

Keya

Lost Love Above 110th Street

Lyrics To A Woman In Harlem

Mother Earth

Mountain Top

Mustard Seed

My Sister

Mystic Eclipse

No-longer

Ocean Dreamer

Of A Goddess's Tears

Penniless Love

R&B Divas

Renaissance Poetry

Selfless

Smothered By Certainty

Sway Like Jazz

That Snow Storm

The Gospel of Her Synoptic Emotions

The Places In My Heart

Two Dreams

Where Are You

LYRICS

TO A WOMAN

IN HARLEM

A Book of Poetry

TYRON MOTIF

A Burning Desire

A burning fire of desire
That love that burns
A flame as raw as a wild beast
In my heart I hold firm

::STIMULATED ON HIGH DANCING IN THE SKY::

The backdrop to our embrace
Wrapped in wings of love
Above the 9th cloud
Surrounded by
…Sun rays…
…Bright stars…
…*And your smile*…

Earnestly desperate for a love
A love ablaze
Burning holes throughout my hard shell
Creating a maze
A maze of light shinning like
The peak of summer days before night

A burning fire of desire
That love that burns
Proposing with a diamond
In my hand I hold firm
An exchange of vows
Your thrown bouquet
A honeymoon on a tropical isle
Making love all day

A FREEDOM THAT

HURT

LIKE HELL

Along with your freedom
You can see
Our love from a distance
You can feel
Its pull above all you refuse
But our freedom pains your heart
Your soul cries out to its companion
To its ir-replace-able mate
(On earth and beyond)
Me...

Because our souls fly free
When we are together
But you wiped its tears
And found freedom apart
A freedom that hurt me like hell
Unlike any other hurt caused by me
My lying

My cheating
My heart is now trapped
And finally you are free

A NEW LOVE

When a new love blocked my vision
I broke down that wall of emotions
And kissed it goodbye

> In central park I walked in search of
> Shade beneath apple trees to write
> Though my vision was *distorted*

As the wrinkled pages in my diary
The road maps of my inner most thoughts
Blind when blank but yet possessing potential

> A potential new love
> A vision I can make use of
> Poetry…My lover
> I kiss her goodbye
> Only to write another

Love, where…
Love, where do we stand?
Can we stand?
Can we ever be…
Ever see…

A future together from here?

From where
I never knew love
You are my
New love

A RELAPSE OF LOVE
AND TEARS

Why do we love so hard?

In silence we cry
And I had a heart
…A love in you
Now we are a p a r t
Without an us
But always with love

In silence we cry
When we are a p a r t
I can hear your tears
Why are we not happy?
Why is love so hard?

In silence we cry
At times without tears
Love on high
We whisper between kisses
We cry in silence

In silence we cry
Without an us
But always in love
Why do we love so hard?
We love 'til death do us apart
We break up to make up
We pray in silence
As we cry
As we make love

ALONE TOGETHER

From my Westside project's window
I watched her as she exited the bus
Aware of my presence she smiled and waved
I released a kiss from my hand
And she blew one straight to my heart

Her long hair flowed down her back
Jet black and relaxed
Blowing in the wind

Soon I heard her
Climbing each step
Higher and higher
Louder and louder

She lived alone as I do
(For different reasons of course)
Death caused her loneliness
I cannot find myself

She was the only lesbian in our building
I protected her with every fiber of my being
Some nights she cooked me dinner

Some days I did her laundry

Death caused her loneliness
Death caused her debts
Because New York state and
Your insurance once said
No baby-girl
No baby-girl

IT WAS ALL JUST SEX

Dedicated to Keisha
Rest beautifully in peace

ASUNDER

How can this ever come to be?

A love now lost
Gone forever so it seems
Forever these days is
As long as my sleeves
Held together by the cuff-links of my heart

Together no longer
A love diminished
I cannot believe we are finished

How can this ever come to be?

I am alone in this house
Gone is the home we built
Built together over the years
In remembrance of us
So I shed these tears

Tears stream down both of my cheeks
And land on the shores of this page
Smearing ink until my words fade

Like you
Like us
Oh I ask

How can this ever come to be?

BEAUTIFUL BLACK
WOMEN

Why are our sisters
Called bitches and hoes?
NEVER beautiful black women

Did Africa thrive on self hatred?
Was every woman there called a bitch?
Or was our respect left
In the bellies of slave ships?
No!

Our ancestors are kings and queens
Who labored endlessly
Without fear
...to dream
...to pray
...to sing

They fought for our freedom
They fought for our lives
Whipped and raped but never lost sight
Still we have lost mind and might

The bitches and hoes must end tonight

YOU ARE BEAUTIFUL BLACK WOMEN

BEYOND EXPRESSION

I love being in this chapel
With believers of God
Their devotion
Their faith
Their relationship with Christ
All of it inspires me

Being in this chapel moves me beyond expression

Here I can still hear
My grandmother's voice
All the wisdom she gave me over the years

She now stands before me
In the form of infinite light
A glow shining bright
Brighter than the rarest diamond

Her widow now stands before me
Depicting the most beautiful portrait
Ever seen by mankind

Being in this chapel moves me beyond expression

All the warnings she gave
All the lessons she taught
All the family stories she told
Were filled with love
And are wrapped around me

Being in this chapel moves me beyond expression

I cried
Dropped to my knees
Bowed and kissed her feet

Then that light disappeared
Just as sudden as it appeared
And there I was
Kissing the ground she walked on

YES!

Being in this chapel moves me beyond expression

Dedicated to the love of my life
Annett Ross

BODY LANGUAGE

I can read you like a book
    I see the world of your emotions
        I feel the energy of your thoughts
          As we make love

I see the horizon's when you cum
    Your body language…
        Gives me a sense of direction
          Your facial expressions…
            Turn me completely on

And when you moan

    It's
        All
          Poetry

BOOBOO LOVE JUICE

(For Tatiana)

Give love to me
Give love to me again
So I may know which world I reside in
Which world I will reside in again

You will awake to my kiss each morning
Each morning to you I will present
A kiss to your lips
A kiss to your hips
A kiss to every inch of your skin

Give love to me
Give love to me again
So I can drink the juice
Of your fountain of love

The reservoir of love liquid
Trickles onto my tongue
As it drips from her pearl
When it rains she pours on my head

Give love to me

Give love to me again
And again…
And again…
And again…
And again…

A love that will love like no other love
A love that will love with no end

BURIED TREASURES
BENEATH HARLEM

Allow me to be buried in your heart
Deep beneath the surface
Where your passions reside
Where your love now hides
Where your happiness lies dormant
(Surely afraid to fly)
Where your fear of being hurt will vanish
Where your fear of being abandoned will die

Bury me deep within your heart
So I may heal that little girl
Who was abused by the world
…So innocent
…So young
…So fragile
…So frail

Bury me deep within your heart
So I can help you rediscover the woman you are
So I can resurrect that deadliness within you
Bury me…

Please, bury me alive
So I can open your eyes
Peel back the disguise
Put your love on high
Kiss your pains goodbye

Please take this shovel
And dig me a hole
A hole so deep
I can stand or sleep
A hole that I can fill with joy
A hole that cannot be breached

COMELINESS ATTRACTION

My affection is intense like myrrh
Beyond a curiosity for her
Beloved passion strong and lovely
Wrapped in my heart warm and snugly
Beautiful love of delight and joy
Who dare not confuse my heart with a toy
Pleasures in pursuit of happiness
Love!

A pain with a magic twist
A high of greatness
Supreme understanding
Emotions' empress with a stimulus
Firm touch yet sensitive

My bliss
Her softness
My hardness
Her heaven

A preferred tenderness

A kiss from my woman friend
And a fondness of her body
Brings change to my day
A hope for true love
A change in my ways
Cherished caress of comfort
It's she I am in love with
Holding dear to a time never to end
A time that always seems to begin
Comeliness attraction

COMPASSIONATE ONE

Your compassion and love is everlasting
I can never do enough of anything You are asking
The Compassionate One
Spreading His wings
Protecting my very being
I love You!
You are The Most High
Above all others
At times I ask why You've chosen me
I do not deserve Your compassionate unfailing love
Yet I pray each day
That You continue to shower me
With Your grace, divine love, protection
And of course
All of Your blessings

DEFIANT LOVE

Oh, what have I become?

What shall I say…
When the contamination
Of thought prevails?
When the monogamy is lost?
When my everything is at home
And I yet travel for more?

A battle between love
And the temptation of lust
Can create emotional sandstorms
Of high winds adrift
Changing the landscape of
The relationship you are in

So free your mind of stagnant beliefs
And open your heart to a new love
Be free of conservative shackles
That wish to dictate who one should love

But love expires when the heart rebels
A defiance of love that seems so frail

When one exhales with resistance
Love will no longer be in existence

So kill me or give me away
Because love isn't enough to make me stay

EMBRACE ME

...Embrace me
Restore a love lost
To you I submit
Hold captive my heart
Love seems far off
Envy is near stalking its pry
What's love without care?

Embrace me...
Without distant smiles
...Embrace me
For I am no longer wild

Embrace me
Embrace me
For I am your child

Embrace me forevermore
For life and beyond
Embrace me for who I am
As days are long
And as nights are cold
For your embrace is warm

...Embrace me
Restore a love lost
Heal a love torn
Let's return to our original form

Embrace me
    Love me
        Hold me
            Chase me

Embrace me...
When I am in need of your help
...Embrace me
As I embrace this expression of self

My inner being pours out as tears do
As pain and love does
In your favorite romance novel

...Embrace me, please
Do not keep your love bottled
Embrace me...
Though some things are hard to swallow
...Embrace me
Because what we have is far from shallow

Embrace me
Embrace me
For I know your heart is not hollow

...Please just embrace me...

ENGAGED WALL FLOWER

Out of sight
Out of mind
I fell out of love
While confined
A lost love in time

Engaged to this wall flower

Like centerfolds of beautiful land
I close my eyes
And stroll in beautiful sand

Engaged to this wall flower
My mind in a trance
Fantasizing about a new love
I just met

I stare at this wall flower
Taped to this prison wall
Above my pillow
Where we both rest

GOODNIGHT
HARLEM

FABRICS OF LOVE
(ON THE HUDSON RIVER)

When we found love

We were on a boat

Staring back at Manhattan

As we drifted

Aimlessly in choppy waters

Firmly embracing

Beneath big mama's quilt

Knitted in the South

Small square-cut pieces

Bound by thread

Thread from each fabric

She obtained over the years

From our ankles to our necks

Her journey north

FOR BEING ME

Love me
For I love you too
Love me
For I will heal your wounds
Love me
Under the sun and moon
For I will love you
Like you have never been loved

Love me
On days when darkness looms
I promise to love you
Until we lay in that tomb
I will love you beyond then
By God's grace I will

Simply love me
For being me
And I will love you
For being you

GOLD TIPS

Harlem jogs each morning to the gym
Her long dreads swing with gold tips
By 5:30am she's sweaty and fit
Feeding her children turkey bacon and grits
Harlem bathes in African pride
Shea butter skin with almond eyes
Harlem views the world as her mother did
No child should be raised a motherless kid

Harlem jogs each morning to the gym
Her long dreads swing with gold tips
Blowing in the wind as kisses
A single mother refusing to be a mistress
Entrepreneur owning her own hair shop
Hanging portraits of her father who was fatally shot
Harlem views the world as her father did
No child should be raised a fatherless kid

Her long dreads with gold tips
A symbol of her strength
Obtaining patience in her
Daily struggle
A virtuous woman

Who knows what love does

She's the one who overcame
And still remains sane
Knowing change
Won't be as smooth as plains
But some things always remain same

When it rains it pours
Leaving her dreads wet
She's celibate but craves
The opposite sex

Her children come first
And the men she met
Can never match up
She's in love with her dreads

See! Here Harlem stands
Not conceitedly
But with self-assurance
She's fierce with zeal
The epitome of a successful woman

Now look her in the eyes!
If you wish, try to

Decipher the elements of her soul
Bear witness to her glow
As the sun shines against snow

Her soul meek, yet vibrant
And speak to every heart
Gentle, yet sharp

Her precious, tranquil presence is pleasant
Her conversation is a blessing
Her message is respected
And receptive as gifts

At a time in a space
Where love collapses
And faith seems obsolete

HARLEM BROWN REMAINS AT PEACE!

HARLEM TEARS

(IN HER VOICE)

I cannot see my future
Through all these tears
The pain that I feel
Put my soul in a stare
Yet I'm not alone
It's remorse and it's fear
I mourn for her too
Yet they say I don't care

I have God in my life
My soul is clean
No grudge against those
Who sold me dreams
So hold me please
Please
Hold me
Squeeze
Please

As I wipe away these tears
And stare into your eyes

HER BEAUTY

I have not seen her since our last visit
Still I cannot forget her beauty
Her round hips thick like my lips
Hers are plump too
With long hair my fingers can run through

I remember her studio apartment
On the East side of Harlem
High times of enjoyment
Her smile
Her tears
Her acting silly
Loud music and wild sex
The fights
The good food
Home alone while she was in school
Still I cannot forget…

I have not seen her since our last visit
But in my prison cell hangs her picture

I CANNOT FORGET HER BEAUTY

KEYA

The memories of Keya
Never leave me
They are my reminders of
Incurred tragedy

When addiction speaks
I turn my ear to her
Listening for her cries for help
We all ignored
Before the suicide

But ashes
Do not speak as loud as addiction
Or memories

LOST LOVE ABOVE 110ᵗʰ STREET

Can a love lost
Be a love we have not met?
A past love that hurt?
A love we all hope for?

Can a love lost
Be the same love we seek?
A love making us weak?
A love breached
Each time one cheats?

A love lost
Or that love we were all
Lost in at some point

A love on high
A love on low
A love that brings pain
A love that warms the soul

Can a love lost

Be a love we have not met?
If so, why do we miss
What we have never had?

A love lost?
Or lost in love?

LYRIC'S TO A WOMAN IN HARLEM

(INSPIRED BY HELENE JOHNSON'S SONNET TO A NEGRO IN HARLEM)

You are royal and majestic

Your mind is your weapon

Your beautiful smile

Your seductive walk

Your dark skin

Your lips so soft

I ponder without understanding

How can beauty be so demanding?

You rise above all in heels and a thong

Head thrown back into the hills with song

Harlem African angel wings spread long

Just as heaven, your passion seems everlasting

Could it be you are God sent?
(*Just asking*)

Why do you feel so sweet?

Why are you so intriguing when you part your teeth?

Wild at home beneath the sheets

A proud black woman on city streets

MOTHER EARTH

(FOR DENISE SIMMONS)

I am bad fruit sprung
From a beautiful tree
Through faith I will be made ripe
By grace I will receive life

And her branches sway
To the winds of her soul

Mother earth
Mother earth

Became a tree of life
Yet she's earth
Day and night

Her love runs as deep as oceans
In her body of land
Her heart is as big as a mountain's
In the garden where she stands

Her roots are buried deep
Beneath her soil

Fertile within her mother's womb
Though my life is full of toil
It's her that I trust

MOTHER EARTH

MOUNTAIN TOP

(TO MY UNBORN DAUGHTER)

From flatland to mountaintop
I watched for months
As earth rose rounding about
A world within a world
A new world awaits
A new world awaits for that day...

She can rob you of purity and joy,
My baby boy...a soldier
Trojan of troy

My sweet precious heaven
Made possible only with a new beginning
A heaven that begins with you

I kiss her birth line
My fingers caress
My palm rotates around her navel
I seek your kicks
Your punches
A kiss

During times of rest
It's those I miss

Your mother's smile warms my heart
Like the whispers of my voice unto you
I speak to my unborn child
As I lay with my ear to her flesh
Our love expressed

Your kick
My touch
Your punch
My kiss

During times of rest
It's those I miss

From flatland to mountaintop
I watched for months

Awaiting that day you can rest on my chest

MUSTARD SEED

She remembers not the broken promises
But cherishes that land of promise
Her strong temple is designed to survive
By grace and good health she's alive
Inspired by her parent's illiteracy
She excelled in Ivy Leagues literally
Her small frame is light as a feather
Carried heavy loads and stormed the weather
With faith the size of a mustard seed
She moved many mountains with ease
A God fearing woman…She loves the lord
Blessed in every way she knows and more
Knowing broken promises hold no weight
Holding dear salvation she knows her fate

MY SISTER

(FOR BIGHEAD)

My sister
Comes with love
Her smile
Sister
Aunt
Mother
Child

My sister
My angel
My sister
Thank you

My sister
Gave birth
A son
Jemeri
Soon he will grow
Big and strong
Until then
He's wrapped
In my sister's arms

My sister
Comes with love
Her smile
Beautiful
Plus
Her child

MYSTIC ECLIPSE

The shadow of our bodies
Against the headboard
Climb the walls until
We are spinning with the ceiling fan
As our love juices rain down
On our naked bodies
In the form of mist
When we kiss
The shadow of our heads form a heart
Against the flickers of candlelight
A love with purpose
A passionate mission
A love with vision
Not blinded by mischief
The oneness of two bodies
Inseparable as we explore
Roaming freely across ebony silk
Creating the most beautiful eclipse

NO-LONGER

No-longer about me
Always about her
I repeat to myself daily
Buried are my past ways
Beneath the soil she walks on
Until beautiful flowers sprout
Washing away her pain
With actual love and happiness
Embraced by us both
Free of unwanted emotions
Obtaining only a handful
Held close to our hearts
Cherished with every breath
And every second together
No-longer about me
Always about her

OCEAN DREAMER
(ON THE EAST RIVER)

Deep and wide and wet, far away, alone
Out on the ocean, sail arms wide and open
Blowing forever! Wishing on a star
Unlike those floating aimlessly as we above our heads
But a star in her, a love I can only dream of

I see a being walking on water
A reflection of me in it
I stand
I reach into night with an open hand
We touch…a familiar touch
A touch I can only dream of

I hold her in my arms as the sail hugs the world
Relaxed and aware, our rhythm, our waves
Her back to my chest, I gaze, amazed
As we drift away to a place unknown
As I dream

The crescent arched like our bodies

As we reach the reflection of sun

My fingers tap dance on the ocean

OF A GODDESS'S TEARS

Of a goddess's tears I speak
Sweet and sour, yummy
Her lover thinks
A love that screams
As tears descend in streams

Of a goddess's tears I see,
Rolling sideways
Onto her pillow moist
Damp, just slightly, where
Her lover's lips were free

Of a goddess's tears I hear,
Melodies of love above
Time square light,
Above commercial flights each night

Of a goddess's tears I speak
Of a goddess's tears I see
Of a goddess's tears I hear

As they fall from her cheeks
And descend through air
Coupled with the tears of her lover
Love juices from both women
And imported wine from France
A Siamese mermaid now swimming

Dedicated to June Jordan
1936-2002

PENNILESS LOVE

My strength evaporated
Like rain drops on a summer day
When you walked out of my life
Today, I now see what I couldn't
Despite my good sight

        Finally, I can admit
        I have done you wrong
        Now I commit to never again
        Bring you harm
        And maintain our love
        With delightful attraction and charm

Love opened my heart
But confined my eyed
To the backside of planks
Where it is uncomfortably dank
With a chill similar to a cold heart
And we both sank

        We are as sick as the things
        We cannot let go.
        And we cannot let go

Of each other
When we are together
You are as sick as I am
When I am alone
Asking why did I let go
I toss and turn without sleep
Making love to resentment
Self-reflective emotions imprisoned
A penniless love of no value
Indifferent? Yes!
An indifference without you

R&B DIVAS

R&B divas
    Lead with attitude
        And never settle for less
           Harlem knows
           Harlem knows
              She's a diva
                And what
she wants in life
                    She
will fight to obtain it

R&B divas
    Fly
    Rockin' the latest fashion
        From heels to hand bags
        European tags
           Cash or plastic
           Dramatic
          (*When it's time for it*)

            Sarcastic

       And you gotta' adore it

H
  A
    R
      L
        E
          M

RENAISSANCE
POETRY CRY

I never met a love with eyes
A love with ears
Yet my love cries
Yet my love hears

Tears of joy
Tears of pain
Tears of love
Each tear is the same

I hear you speak
Love and heartbeats
Though love can make a man weak
It's you…Strong, yet sweet

So to you I blow kisses
Even when they are unseen
My thoughts…Your wishes
Your smile…My dreams

I never met a love with eyes

A love with ears
Yet my love cries
Yet my love hears

Tonight I will cry
Or write poetry
Or lose my mind
Or listen to jazz
Or hip hop
Or listen to a child's cries at birth
As my emotion's flip-flop

Tonight I will cry
Or write poetry
Or lose my mind
Or dance
Or paint
Or perform spoken word
As I cry like I've lost my mind

SELFLESS

All week I searched for bright stars
But that storm above all blocked my vision
Though my heart still sees a future
And the storm moved out to sea
My third eye says no, but love makes me weak

When we eat your favorites, I enjoy your smile
When you cum, I smile too
We kiss while sweaty
Then sleep on wet sheets
And dream we are out dining
Cracking jokes on the waitress
As we look at the menu

Sometimes I push you away
It hurts
I am familiar with a broken heart
As mine was for years

We rescued one another
From our own sorrowful dissension
I know of no love without you
So I chose you for my own

DESIRES
PAIN
PASSIONS
LOVE
LIFE

SMOTHERED BY CERTAINTY

When she is smothered by certainty
In the hour of revelation
She will know absolute peace
The opposite of loneliness
A love unconditional for certain

I have slept with dead flowers
She who blooms but never prospers
Broken by fragile love, numb to pain
A pain unbearable when alone
A pain ignored when she is home

Love made intense when tension at its peak
I am lost with her…Un-found without her
Asking what is life without faith in the unseen

Imagining what you would want a person to be
Compared to the one you love
With character defects making the experience real
So intriguing like butterflies in your stomach
The moment you hear my voice

Her dreams forever on replay each day awake
Each breath she takes asleep
Each dream she wishes to be
That life she wishes to live

A husband
A home
And kids

When she is smothered by certainty
In the hour of revelation
She will know absolute peace
The opposite of loneliness
A love unconditional for certain

SWAY LIKE JAZZ

Harlem sways
Like blues
Sways like jazz
Sways to her own tune
Oh Harlem bad

Uptown girl
Head held high
As Harlem sways
To a tune gone bye
Grace
Class
Oh Harlem bad

Sways like blues
Sways like jazz
Uptown girl
Uptown girl
Head held high

All women
Sweet like pie
With a sway

That makes
Grown men cry

THAT SNOW STORM

During that snow storm your birthday arrived
With candles and a power outage in Harlem
We were in the midst of our own storm
Stuck in our own ruts
Like your car tires spinning in front of my house
Going nowhere fast

You always returned to the same place
Our love started
Where the pain came and went so often
We began to disregard it

I hit my bottom with addiction
You up lifted and carried me
Though I was a heavy load
Your love kept us warm
When days were cold
Like my heart at times
Often like my actions
Just like that snow storm...
Then I got arrested
We faded to black
While our candles burned out

THE GOSPEL OF HER
SYNOPTIC EMOTIONS

Do regret and shame coexist?
Where honesty and truth become synoptic
Yet less comprehensive in common view?

To confide in one's trust or reveal
What is capaciously dear to your heart

A burden lifted
Emotional release
A pain relief
Momentarily free

As the synoptic gospels
As one are our emotions
As Matthew, Mark and Luke described
Their accounts run deep as oceans
Just as our special bond
What we share goes as deep as those
In this union of love we both founded
Still you are silent
Dwelling in a past I am aware of

Which only magnifies your unawareness
Of who I truly am
And the unconditional love my heart
Obtained for you
Still I live by the synoptic gospels of her emotions
Still I love you despite your past
I have my own as we all do
As the sun shines down on earth
At the peak of day
Baby, I adore you

So why spread your oppressive distress
By the concealment of your own truth?
Where honesty has no home
Evicted by a clandestine motive

Now with regret
Squat with your chin in your chest
Full of shame or regrets
That give way to pleasures from within

Where love, communication, orgasms, and trust
Produce magical moments that
She prays will never diminish or become tarnished
By the resurrection of her past

Still I ask

Do regret and shame coexist?
Where honesty and truth become synoptic
Yet less comprehensive in common view?

THE PLACES IN MY HEART

I am a romantic with a heart
And a million mistakes
The *motif* of her life
Symphonies of love
Making love in every place
The place is in my heart

> Every place…
> Every dream…
> Every heartbeat…
> Together by hope
> A hope for a future
> Together like rope

Symphonies of love
Your smile
Your cries
As we kiss
Wiping tears from your eyes
Shhh!
Listen to the music in every place

The place is in my heart

Our paths cross like the blood
Of our unborn child
Our body fluids
When we are making love
Creating waves as vibrant as drugs
Crashing the shores of tranquility in every place
The place is in my heart

The day we exchange vows
The world as we know it
Will be changed forever
Your rose will bloom as always
As your legs spread wide comfortably
The night of our honey moon

I bury my face deep within your love
Which contains
Every hope…
Every desire…
Every dream…
Every note of…
Every slow love making symphony

My tongue dances
To the rhythm
Of your hips
As my lips
Two step in every place
The place is in my heart

TWO DREAMS

(FOR INCARCERATED WOMEN)

Gander eyes roam
Quick and swift
Comparing two opposites
A simile without speaking

Like a ghetto sluice
When the levee broke
Tears flow downstream
Puddles on letters they wrote

Smote then smite now
She writes of her own feelings
Alone
Staring at her cell ceiling

An abortion before the pregnancy
Apprehension after release
Relapse once clean
Her nightmares once dreams

Now only two dreams remain
To become free

To become a published writer

So she writes from prison

WHERE ARE YOU?

MOTHER WHERE ARE YOU?

Confined in a state of bondage by addiction
The cause and symptoms of struggles endured
Yet I adore my children through it all

DAUGHTER WHERE ARE YOU?

Confined in a state of bondage
He is heavy handed
And abuse arrives with his liquor bottle
The size of the Atlantic

SISTER WHERE ARE YOU?

Confined in a state of bondage
Where the flesh around my arm's wrist
Has been eaten away by handcuffs too tight
Squeezing life out of my sleepless nights
My palms are numb like jelly
Unable to rub my belly

Lyrics To A Woman In Harlem

As my unborn child kick

HARLEM

Acknowledgments

Adrienne Horn Editor
Tanya Harris Author (Publish preparation Adviser)
Roosevelt Public Library
Central Station
Clothing Store
Philly Street Poets
Hempstead Public Library
Jay Allan Radio Show
Rocok Radio Show
Timothy J Ravenell (Spiritual Adviser)
Nick Wilson (Vibes and Verses)
Ujima James (Nassau County Chapter of the National Action
Network)
Loli's Soul Food
Poetess Elle McLin (WWW.ellenmclin.com)
Janae Poetic Soul Stewart
Cappadonna (Wu-Radio)
Poet Hall in Eerie Pennsylvania
Luff House Philly
Harold Branch (Triumph Of Children)
Denise Simmons
George Simmons
Terrence Turner
Christopher Simmons
Calvin Ross
Nettie Graham
Tatiana Abel
Francis Abel

Pastor Derek Price
Risa Wright
Christopher Mustafa Horton
Ty Gray-EL
Nicole Graham
April Diane
Luchetta Manus
Lady Lawless (Lady Mason)
D Christopher Harvey
Kristi Black
Sapphire McGhee
Annjell Robert Author
MzHotness
Keith Murry
Micaal Stevens

About The Author

Tyron Motif, poet, spoken word artist, and motivational speaker, was born as Tyron Ross on the 27th of June in 1983 in Roosevelt, Long Island. He penned the majority of his first poetic work entitled **Lyrics to a Woman in Harlem** while he was incarcerated. He was released from prison on July 17, 2013.

He currently spends his time performing at open mic events and working with at-risk youth in New York. He currently lives with his children, Tyron and Tymir, and his sweetheart, Tatiana. In the near future, he hopes to publish his second book of poetry as well as his first fiction novel.

AUTHOR TYRON MOTIF